MILITARY MACHINES

FIGHTER JETS

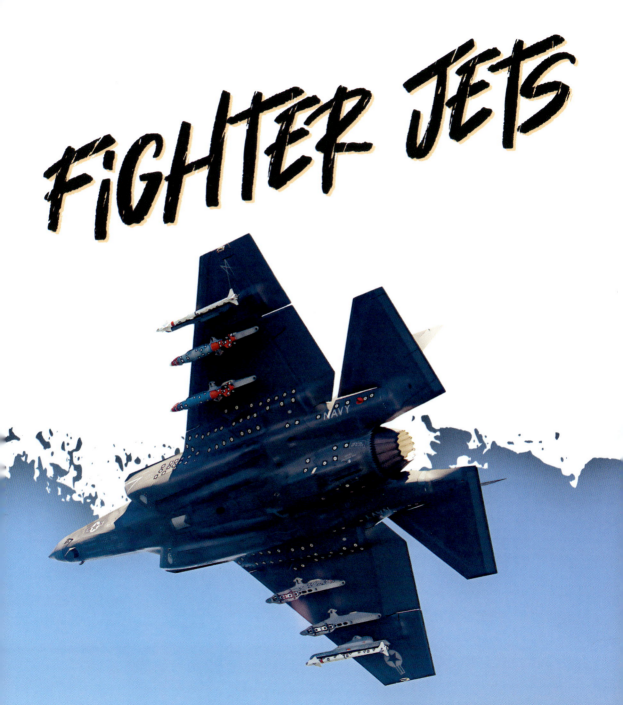

BY CHARLES MARLIN

WWW.APEXEDITIONS.COM

Copyright © 2025 by Apex Editions, Mendota Heights, MN 55120. All rights reserved. No part of this book may be reproduced or utilized in any form or by any means without written permission from the publisher.

Apex is distributed by North Star Editions:
sales@northstareditions.com | 888-417-0195

Produced for Apex by Red Line Editorial.

Photographs ©: Senior Airman Taylor Crul/US Air Force/DVIDS, cover; Dane Wiedmann/DVIDS, 1, 16–17; Senior Airman Zachary Bumpus/US Air Force, 4–5; Staff Sgt. Tony R. Tolley/US Air Force, 6–7; Brad White/US Air Force, 8; Todd Cromar/US Air Force/DVIDS, 9; Hulton Archive/Getty Images, 10–11; Department of Defense/US Air Force, 12; J. M. Eddins Jr./US Air Force, 13, 29; South Korean Defense Ministry/AP Images, 14–15; Airman 1st Class Mason Hargrove/US Air Force/DVIDS, 18; Senior Airman Erica Webster/US Air Force/DVIDS, 19; US Navy/AP Images, 20–21; Tech. Sgt. John Raven/US Air Force/DVIDS, 22–23; Christopher Furlong/Getty Images News/Getty Images, 24–25; Senior Airman Benjamin Sutton/DVIDS, 26–27

Library of Congress Control Number: 2024940142

ISBN
979-8-89250-337-2 (hardcover)
979-8-89250-375-4 (paperback)
979-8-89250-447-8 (ebook pdf)
979-8-89250-413-3 (hosted ebook)

Printed in the United States of America
Mankato, MN
012025

NOTE TO PARENTS AND EDUCATORS

Apex books are designed to build literacy skills in striving readers. Exciting, high-interest content attracts and holds readers' attention. The text is carefully leveled to allow students to achieve success quickly. Additional features, such as bolded glossary words for difficult terms, help build comprehension.

TABLE OF CONTENTS

CHAPTER 1
Fight in the Sky 4

CHAPTER 2
History 10

CHAPTER 3
Types of Fighters 16

CHAPTER 4
Flying High 22

COMPREHENSION QUESTIONS • 28
GLOSSARY • 30
TO LEARN MORE • 31
ABOUT THE AUTHOR • 31
INDEX • 32

CHAPTER 1

Fight in the Sky

A fighter jet speeds through the air. The pilot checks his **radar**. It shows two enemy fighters nearby. The pilot shoots one down with a **missile**.

The F-15 Eagle is a fighter jet. It can fly nearly 1,900 miles per hour (3,100 km/h).

The other enemy plane keeps coming. It fires a heat-seeking missile. The first pilot shoots a **flare**. The enemy missile hits it.

Fighters shoot flares and then turn sharply. Missiles hit the flares instead of the planes.

AVOIDING MISSILES

Flares give off heat. So, they can trick heat-seeking missiles. But some missiles use radar. To avoid that type, fighters can let out metal strips. These strips confuse the radar. It can't find the right **target**.

Then, the pilot shoots the enemy plane's wing. It catches fire. The enemy pilot **ejects**. She uses a parachute. Her plane crashes into the ground.

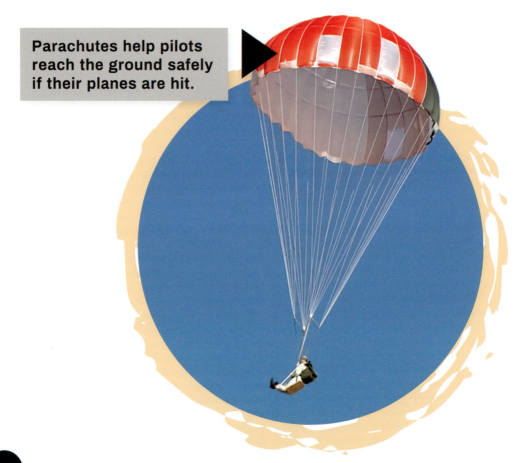

Parachutes help pilots reach the ground safely if their planes are hit.

FAST FACT Some fighter guns can fire 100 rounds per second.

Many fighter guns use large 25-mm rounds.

CHAPTER 2

History

Militaries first used planes for battle in World War I (1914–1918). The planes were made from wood and cloth. They carried small machine guns.

Close-range battles between planes are called dogfights.

Militaries used metal fighters in World War II (1939–1945). After the war, people added jet engines. Fighters became faster. And they carried more **weapons**.

The P-47 Thunderbolt was a powerful World War II fighter. It carried several tons of fuel and weapons.

The F-86D Sabre was the first fighter to carry missiles.

FAST FACT

After World War II, fighters began carrying missiles. Missiles were more **accurate** and powerful than guns.

After being dropped by a fighter, a GBU-12 bomb can fly 6 miles (9.7 km) to its target.

Aiming at targets became more difficult in fast planes. So, people added technology to help pilots. Radar helped find enemies. Guided missiles could track enemies.

COMPUTERS

Today, computers often help pilots. Computers can complete basic tasks. Then pilots can focus on harder tasks. For example, computers can warn pilots about incoming enemies. Pilots then decide what to do next.

CHAPTER 3

TYPES OF FIGHTERS

Today, militaries use several types of fighters. Interceptors attack incoming enemies. They use guns and missiles to take down planes.

An F-35 fighter jet can carry up to 18,000 pounds (8,000 kg) of weapons.

Night fighters have powerful radar. They also have sensors that detect heat. These tools show the fighter's surroundings. They help pilots fly in the dark.

Flying at night can be risky. Pilots must have extra practice for these kinds of flights.

F-22 Raptors are stealth fighters. Their powerful engines and sleek shape help them fly quickly.

SNEAKY FIGHTERS

Stealth fighters can hide from radar. They have thick paint. It takes in radio waves. They also have curved surfaces. These angles bounce radio waves away.

Other types of fighters can fly far. They may go deep into enemy land. There, they can attack enemy fighters or drop bombs.

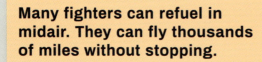
Many fighters can refuel in midair. They can fly thousands of miles without stopping.

FAST FACT

Some fighters can fly nearly 2,500 miles (4,000 km) without refueling.

CHAPTER 4

FLYING HIGH

Several fighters often work together. They may fly in shapes called formations. Some of the planes attack enemies. Others **protect** the attackers.

Fighters may use a formation that looks like the letter V.

Pilots must be quick in battle. They can make sharp turns and dives. These moves make planes harder for missiles to follow.

RADAR SCREENS

Displays in the cockpit show radar information. Friendly aircraft are green circles. Enemies are red triangles. Pilots can lock on to the enemy to fire a missile.

Fighters may do rolls or loops to avoid being hit.

Some fighters carry two people. The second person helps control the weapons.

A fighter pilot uses a control stick to steer the plane. The pilot uses a throttle to control a plane's speed. These parts also have buttons for sensors and weapons.

FAST FACT
A control stick's buttons often have different shapes and **textures**. Pilots can tell them apart by feel.

COMPREHENSION QUESTIONS

Write your answers on a separate piece of paper.

1. Write a few sentences describing the main ideas of Chapter 3.

2. Would you like to fly in a fighter jet? Why or why not?

3. When were fighter planes first used for battle?
   A. during World War I
   B. during World War II
   C. after World War II

4. How would different-shaped buttons make a control stick easier to use?
   A. Pilots would not have to use the control stick.
   B. Pilots could tell the buttons apart without looking at them.
   C. Pilots would not have to steer the plane.

5. What does **confuse** mean in this book?

*These strips **confuse** the radar. It can't find the right target.*

    A. make something easy to understand
    B. make something hard to understand
    C. make something sound louder

6. What does **complete** mean in this book?

*Today, computers often help pilots. Computers can **complete** basic tasks.*

    A. finish
    B. fail at
    C. hide from

Answer key on page 32.

GLOSSARY

accurate

Able to hit a target that is being aimed at.

ejects

Pops out of a plane so a person can escape.

flare

A device that can create a bright and hot flame.

missile

An object that is shot or launched as a weapon.

protect

To keep something or someone safe.

radar

A system that sends out radio waves to locate objects.

target

A person, place, or object that people plan to attack.

textures

How things feels when touched.

weapons

Things that are used to cause harm.

TO LEARN MORE

BOOKS

Gaertner, Meg. *US Air Force*. Mendota Heights, MN: Apex Editions, 2023.

Hamilton, S. L. *The World's Fastest Planes*. Minneapolis: Abdo Publishing, 2021.

McKinney, Donna. *F-22 Raptor*. Minneapolis: Bellwether Media, 2024.

ONLINE RESOURCES

Visit **www.apexeditions.com** to find links and resources related to this title.

ABOUT THE AUTHOR

Charles Marlin is an author, editor, and avid cyclist. He lives in rural Iowa.

INDEX

C
cockpit, 24
computers, 15
controls, 26–27

F
flares, 6–7
formations, 22

I
interceptors, 16

J
jet engines, 12

M
missiles, 4, 6–7, 13, 15, 16, 24

N
night fighters, 18

R
radar, 4, 7, 15, 18–19, 24

S
sensors, 18, 26
stealth fighters, 19

W
weapons, 12, 26
World War I, 10
World War II, 12–13

ANSWER KEY:
1. Answers will vary; 2. Answers will vary; 3. A; 4. B; 5. B; 6. A